The Midlands

Edited By Jess Giaffreda

First published in Great Britain in 2019 by:

Young Writers
Remus House
Coltsfoot Drive
Peterborough
PE2 9BF
Telephone: 01733 890066
Website: www.youngwriters.co.uk

All Rights Reserved
Book Design by Spencer Hart
© Copyright Contributors 2019
SB ISBN 978-1-78988-513-2
Printed and bound in the UK by BookPrintingUK
Website: www.bookprintinguk.com
YB0405E

Foreword

Dear Reader,

Are you ready to explore the wonderful delights of poetry?

Young Writers' *Poetry Patrol* gang set out to encourage and ignite the imaginations of 5-7 year-olds as they took their first steps into the magical world of poetry. With **Riddling Rabbit**, **Acrostic Croc** and **Sensory Skunk** on hand to help, children were invited to write an acrostic, sense poem or riddle on any theme, from people to places, animals to objects, food to seasons. *Poetry Patrol* is also a great way to introduce children to the use of poetic expression, including onomatopoeia and similes, repetition and metaphors, acting as stepping stones for their future poetic journey.

All of us here at Young Writers believe in the importance of inspiring young children to produce creative writing, including poetry, and we feel that seeing their own poem in print will keep that creative spirit burning brightly and proudly.

We hope you enjoy reading this wonderful collection as much as we enjoyed reading all the entries.

Contents

Barlborough Primary School, Barlborough

Charlotte Sorby (5)	1
Luke Slater (5)	2
Blake Newton Phillips (6)	3
Elizabeth (6)	4
Isaac (5)	5
Millie Lord (5)	6
Lily-Mae Hill (5)	7
Ivy Ogden (5)	8
Thomas Newbould (5)	9
Holly Georgia Luxton (6)	10
Phoebe Allen (5)	11
William Swift (5)	12
Eduard Ionut Spataru (6)	13
Kezia Elliott (6)	14
Oscar Storey (5)	15

Broad Heath Community Primary School, Coventry

Elen Moghos (7)	16
Amanah Sabir (7)	17
Jasmine Masih (6)	18

Holme Valley Primary School, Bottesford

Lewis Johnson (5)	19
Kasper G Shaw (5)	20
Rajin Jenopan (5)	21
William Pearson (6)	22
Miles Brocklesby (5)	23
Freddie Stevenson (6)	24

Oak Tree Primary Academy, Mansfield

Jasmin Carlin (6)	25
Ruby Quincey (7)	26
Ruby Morrison (7)	28
Macie Mellors (7)	29
Ellie-May McCullagh (7)	30
Aaliyah-Ann Smith (7)	31
Robert John Radford (7)	32
Kayden Finch (7)	33
Noah Skeavington (7)	34
Lucy Marshall (6)	35
Leece Hickling (7)	36
Charli Buck (7)	37
Casey Lennon (7)	38
Charlie-Lucas Koperski-Stewart (7)	39
Katie-Leigh Hardy (6)	40
Georgia Ingram (6)	41
Amelia Hassan (7)	42
Jensen Charlton (7)	43
Lilith Smith	44
Jessica Parker (6)	45
Caleb Thompson (7)	46
Ivy May Simpson (5)	47
Keogh Turner (7)	48
Aiko Hallam (6)	49
Phoebe Marie Barnett (6)	50
Jaycee-Mae Vaughan (6)	51
Alfie Rowley (5)	52
Henri-Lee O'Neill (6)	53
Reece Simpson (6)	54
Kaiden Radford (6)	55
April Marshall (6)	56
Ethan O'Shea (5)	57

Liara Townsend (5)	58
Adam Hassan (6)	59

Portway Infant School, Allestree

Sam Knifton (7)	60
Caitlin Louise O'Reilly (6)	61
Henry Greenhalgh (7)	62
Christos Serghi (6)	63
Elizabeth Ellen Hancox (7)	64
Lily White (6)	65
Leo Spencer (6)	66
Jack Thomas Flint (6)	67
Oliver Curr (6)	68

St Edward's Catholic Academy, Swadlincote

Ribljot Kaur (6)	69
Amelie Struggles (6)	70
Charlie Gardner (5)	71
Charlie Mole (6)	72
Lydia Cox (6)	73
Bella Saddington (6)	74
Annemarie O'Brien (5)	75
Dollie Hutton (6)	76
Layla Hallam (6)	77
Jason Alexander Ogunlana (5)	78
Evie-Rose Morgan (5)	79
Oliver Czarkowski (6)	80
Pixie Eyre (6)	81
Aaron Cox (5)	82

St Thomas More Catholic Primary School, Kettering

Olivia Chacko (6)	83
Jessica Joseph (6)	84
Maizie Ielapi (7)	85
Christa Bijumon (6)	86
Sienna Palmiero (6)	87
Rosemaria Jiju (6)	88
Gerard Rony (7)	89
Grace Claypole (7)	90

Camron Gerard Mills (7)	91
Betsy Flannigan (7)	92
Luke Rahman (7)	93
Oliver Kopaniecki (6)	94
Amelia Jino (7)	95
Aurelia Curtis (6)	96
Sean Prendergast (7)	97
Amelia Alexander (7)	98
Esha Rijo Joseph (6)	99
Matilda Vincitore-Jackson (6)	100
Oscar Arden-Taylor (7)	101
William Richardson (6)	102
Cyprian Leatherland (6)	103
Seth James Stanyon (7)	104
Lily Driscoll (6)	105
Joel Binoy (6)	106
Maria Mucaj (6)	107
Mia Drappo (7)	108
Mini Holder (6)	109
Oliver Wise (7)	110

Sutherland Primary Academy, Blurton

Lottie Tyler (6)	111
Zachary S (6)	112
Ethan Morris (5)	113
Lacey-Mae S (5)	114
Poppy C (5)	115
John V (6)	116
Adam W (6)	117
Aiden B (6)	118
Brooke R (5)	119
Emily F (5)	120
Harry William Shaw (5)	121
Oliver Lawrence (5)	122
Lilly H R (5)	123
Tala H (6)	124
Jaxon P (6)	125
Rory G (5)	126
Jayden Derek Bennett (5)	127
Charlie W (6)	128
Riley O'Connell (6)	129
Ruby (5)	130

Amelia E (6)	131
Emmanuel Chiagozelam U (6)	132
Lilly Iris Bowman (6)	133
Leo G (5)	134
Jenson-Edward L (6)	135
Trystan A (6)	136
Karolina Kovacovska (6)	137
Jacob Heath-Willis (5)	138
Harrison G (5)	139
Zakariya H (5)	140
Stanley William-Booth Cook (6)	141

West Heath Primary School, West Heath

Sophie Stamp-Broadway (6)	142
Lily Grace Fay (6)	143
Mollie Johnson (6)	144
Katie Irene Tonks (7)	145
Kyle Smith (6)	146
Lexi Painter (7)	147
Rehan Ahmed (7)	148

Yardley Wood Community Primary School, Yardley Wood

Sophie Mafuamba (5)	149
Kenzie Taylor (6)	150
Lillie Evans (6)	151
Hunaida Suwan (6)	152
Mohammed Hussnain (6)	153
Dexter Hollingsworth (6)	154
Isla Burton (5)	155
Ibraheem Farrell (5)	156
Toby Page (6)	157
Salah-Eddin Melloul (6)	158
Laibaah Khan (5)	159
Kaéson Gaye-Smith (6)	160
Paige Lake (6)	161
Ethan Hourihan (5)	162
Rylee Mottram (5)	163

Yorkmead School, Hall Green

Saaliha Mahmood (6)	164
Haseeb Abdul (7)	165

The Poems

Winter Senses

I can see snowflakes and sparkly lights,
I can smell sweet hot chocolate
and gingerbread men,
I can taste snowflakes dripping
on my tongue and icicles,
I can feel cold snow and gloves,
I can hear people crunching in the snow
and Christmas bells.

Charlotte Sorby (5)
Barlborough Primary School, Barlborough

Winter Wonderland

I can see glittery snowflakes and snow,
I can smell sweet gingerbread
and Christmas pudding,
I can taste hot chocolate
and Christmas pudding,
I can feel icicles and wet snow,
I can hear wet icicles
and Christmas pudding.

Luke Slater (5)
Barlborough Primary School, Barlborough

Winter Wonderland

I can see glittery fireworks
and dripping icicles,
I can smell gingerbread men and holly,
I can taste gingerbread
and Christmas pudding,
I can feel snow and trees,
I can hear bells and crunchy snow.

Blake Newton Phillips (6)
Barlborough Primary School, Barlborough

Dripping Icicles

I can see glittering snow and icicles,
I can smell hot chocolate
And gingerbread men,
I can taste snowflakes and icicles,
I can feel glittering snow and snowflakes,
I can hear wind and Christmas pudding.

Elizabeth (6)
Barlborough Primary School, Barlborough

Winter Wonderland

I can see snow and dripping icicles,
I can smell hot chocolate
and gingerbread men,
I can taste icicles and hot Christmas dinner,
I can feel white snow and icicles,
I can ear wind and dripping icicles.

Isaac (5)
Barlborough Primary School, Barlborough

Winter Senses

I can see snow and snowflakes,
I can smell hot chocolate
And gingerbread men,
I can taste lollipops and Christmas dinner,
I can feel air and snow,
I can hear Christmas music and jingle bells.

Millie Lord (5)
Barlborough Primary School, Barlborough

Winter Snowflakes

I can see snowflakes
and gingerbread men,
I can smell hot chocolate
and gingerbread men,
I can feel wind,
I can feel snowflakes,
I can hear the birds singing
And I can see snowflakes.

Lily-Mae Hill (5)
Barlborough Primary School, Barlborough

Winter Wonderland

I can see icicles and snowmen,
I can smell hot chocolate
And gingerbread men,
I can taste snowballs and ice,
I can feel snow and hot lights,
I can hear sleighs in the snow and dripping.

Ivy Ogden (5)
Barlborough Primary School, Barlborough

A Winter Poem

I can see snowflakes and icicles,
I can smell gingerbread men and sweets,
I can taste hot chocolate
And Christmas dinner,
I can feel snow and flakes,
I can hear snow and wind.

Thomas Newbould (5)
Barlborough Primary School, Barlborough

Winter Lollipops

I can see melting snow and lollipops,
I can smell gingerbread men and lollipops,
I can taste snow and lollipops,
I can feel snow and lollipops,
I can hear snow and bells.

Holly Georgia Luxton (6)
Barlborough Primary School, Barlborough

Winter Senses

I can see icicles and presents,
I can smell hot chocolate and lollipops,
I can taste Christmas dinner and pudding,
I can feel snow and ice,
I can hear Rudolph and Santa.

Phoebe Allen (5)
Barlborough Primary School, Barlborough

Cold Winter

I can see people throwing snow,
I can smell lollipops and mince pies,
I can taste hot chocolate and snow,
I can feel houses and birds,
I can hear wind and gas.

William Swift (5)
Barlborough Primary School, Barlborough

Senses

I can see people and slides,
I can smell hot chocolate and snow,
I can taste sweets and raindrops,
I can feel the wind and paper,
I can hear cows and horses.

Eduard Ionut Spataru (6)
Barlborough Primary School, Barlborough

Winter Wind

I can see snow and water,
I can smell gingerbread men,
I can taste dinner and snow,
I can feel wet snow,
I can hear cars and drums.

Kezia Elliott (6)
Barlborough Primary School, Barlborough

Winter Wonderland

I can see snow falling,
I can smell strawberries,
I can taste apples,
I can feel wet snow,
I can hear drums.

Oscar Storey (5)
Barlborough Primary School, Barlborough

Being On The Beach

B eing on the beach is fun, the sun is shining brightly in the sky
E verything looks brilliant, watching the seagulls fly
A mazing things all around us, everyone having fun at the beach, making fantastic sandcastles
C heeky seagulls swooping all around us, trying to eat our yummy food
H aving an amazing day at the beach is fun because everything around us is delightful to see.

Elen Moghos (7)
Broad Heath Community Primary School, Coventry

Seaside Dream

I dreamt I went to the seaside one day,
Time to relax and time to play
There were...
Ten silly seagulls,
Nine crabs clicking,
Eight super sandcastles,
Seven bouncy beachballs,
Six windy windmills,
Five brilliant boats,
Four lazy lifeguards,
Three incredible ice creams,
Two lonely lifeboats,
One scorching sun.

Amanah Sabir (7)
Broad Heath Community Primary School, Coventry

Winter Magic
A diamante poem

Snowman,
Cold, freezing
Dancing, singing, twirling
Snowflakes, snowballs, icicles, birds
Falling, swirling, shining,
Dazzling, pretty,
Winter.

Jasmine Masih (6)
Broad Heath Community Primary School, Coventry

Once There Was A Chocolate Room

Once there was a chocolate room,
Full of yummy sweets
Owned by Mr Wonka,
There were lots of different treats!
There were candy canes and lollipops
And gummy bears as well
I hope to go to that chocolate room
Very, very soon
I'd like to taste those
yummy, yummy sweets
In that marvellous chocolate room.

Lewis Johnson (5)
Holme Valley Primary School, Bottesford

I Taste Sweet

You bake me in a cake,
You might stir me into your porridge,
I could be white, milk or dark,
I am sometimes hot and wet,
You could even put marshmallows on me,
Santa might bring you some coins,
Grandma might bring some from M&S,
You can stick me in ice cream
What am I?

Answer: Chocolate.

Kasper G Shaw (5)
Holme Valley Primary School, Bottesford

Fastest Animal

I live in the jungle,
I eat people and animals,
I have yellow skin and black spots,
I can run very fast,
I can run faster than a lion,
I can scare people,
I have a long tail,
I have big, sharp teeth,
I have sharp claws
What am I?

Answer: A cheetah.

Rajin Jenopan (5)
Holme Valley Primary School, Bottesford

The King Of The Arctic

I live in the North Pole,
I have white fur to keep me warm,
I live on the top of the world,
I eat seals, berries and reindeer,
I am the biggest carnivore,
I eat fish too,
I would rather run away than fight,
I am scary
What am I?

Answer: A polar bear.

William Pearson (6)
Holme Valley Primary School, Bottesford

Rocky The Cat

R olling around, warm and snuggly
O ver the fence, he jumps so high!
C heese and ham are his favourite foods
K eeps me company on the walk to school
Y awning after a long day chasing birds.

Miles Brocklesby (5)
Holme Valley Primary School, Bottesford

What Am I?

I roar very loud,
I have sharp teeth,
I have black stripes,
I have orange fur,
I am bigger than a lion
What am I?

Answer: A tiger.

Freddie Stevenson (6)
Holme Valley Primary School, Bottesford

The Roaring Lion

The lions look very soft, they feel furry,
A lion looks calm
They sound very loud
They feel soft and furry
Their fur smells stinky
They taste horrible food
And the blood tastes horrible
Lions are the strongest animals in the jungle
Lions are very, very scary
Lions have a very big mane,
That is soft to touch.
The lions look very soft, they feel furry,
A lion looks like a big calm
They sound very loud
They feel soft and furry
Their fur smells stinky.

Jasmin Carlin (6)
Oak Tree Primary Academy, Mansfield

The Leopard's Jungle Adventure

I see other leopards
that are in my leopard clan,
Hunting some violent prey
I hear leopards running after zebra
And parrots squeaking...
I taste my prey to see if I like it or not
But my favourite are gazelles
I feel their fur and rip their fur,
I can smell delicious meat, that's lion's guts
I can see a little zebra walking,
but will I catch it?
I look like I'm the queen
and my dazzling spots look like
They're going to change colour
I look like I could also catch a tiger

My spots are big
and my legs are skinny and strong!

Ruby Quincey (7)
Oak Tree Primary Academy, Mansfield

The Cheeky Cheetah Adventure

Cheetahs can see a big, open space
With yellow, short grass so they can run fast
They can usually hear other animals
so they have to be very quiet!
They are usually silent too
but can make a roar!
They touch the tickly grass
and feel the scorching sun
They can smell other animals
to eat for their dinner
They are quite lazy,
they lie in the scorching sun,
But then they can sense prey,
They run as fast as they can to catch it!

Ruby Morrison (7)
Oak Tree Primary Academy, Mansfield

The Scary, Spotted Hyena

A spotted hyena has big ears
and spots all over its body,
Hyenas can run fast, super fast,
The hyena can hear a wolf howling,
The hyena can smell disgusting smells,
The hyena can taste
some blood of a tasty frog,
The hyena can touch the crunchy grass,
He runs really quickly,
then lies in the crunchy grass
Then he rolls over.

Macie Mellors (7)
Oak Tree Primary Academy, Mansfield

The Fluffy Flamingo

F lamingoes are majestic, elegant and royal
L ike a big, pink parrot
A flamingo is very soft
M aybe they might splash you!
I think flamingoes are interesting
N ame an animal more special
G reat how they can stand on one leg
O h, their feathers are outrageously beautiful!

Ellie-May McCullagh (7)
Oak Tree Primary Academy, Mansfield

Elephant

E lephants are big, grey and
L ovely and beautiful because they are huge
E lephants
P *lod, plod, plod!*
H igh up
A n elephant is ginormous compared to a snake
N is for their big nose which is a trunk
T he trunk sucks up water and squirt, squirt, squirt!

Aaliyah-Ann Smith (7)
Oak Tree Primary Academy, Mansfield

The Stomping Elephant's Day

Elephants can smell stripy tigers,
Elephants can see brown trees,
Elephants can hear the loud roars of lions,
Elephants can touch green grass
They can feel their little baby's leg,
They can reach the leaves so that the baby
Can play with the leaves nicely
They were really tired after this long day.

Robert John Radford (7)
Oak Tree Primary Academy, Mansfield

The Amazing Warthog!

Warthogs have big, white horns
and eyes that can see so much
They love to swim in dirty water
and feel the warmth around them
They smell horrible,
like they've been rolling in dung!
Yummy bugs and beetles
are their favourite food
They are scared of hearing a trumpet
from an elephant!

Kayden Finch (7)
Oak Tree Primary Academy, Mansfield

The Roar From The Lion

The fierce lion was stomping
through the spiky grass,
And looking for some prey
By sniffing the desert air
He caught the prey
He would dig out the guts
and the scared prey would scream
He went back home to the dark cave
And roared down from there
He went to sleep, roaring around meanly.

Noah Skeavington (7)
Oak Tree Primary Academy, Mansfield

The Loudest Roar

The lion has to find meat,
And the lion goes home to eat the meat
The lion is fluffy
And it has gone sharp claws,
And they are sharp
The lion hears a roar
And it was a different lion
The lion had a baby cub
And the baby had a cute, little nose
But in real life, it is scary.

Lucy Marshall (6)
Oak Tree Primary Academy, Mansfield

The Black Panther

P anthers are black and grey
A ny prey had better start running
N ight hunting for meat and a big meal
T he treetop is where he sees
H is prey
E is for every single day he hunts
R is for running on the plain.

Leece Hickling (7)
Oak Tree Primary Academy, Mansfield

The Leaping Lion

I can see a lion killing its prey,
I can smell a lot of blood
And bones from a lion's prey,
A male lion and a lioness
Might taste some more bones too
They growl to catch their prey
And they might feel
Some bumps on the ground.

Charli Buck (7)
Oak Tree Primary Academy, Mansfield

My Senses Jungle Poem

I can see a swamp full of flamingos,
I can smell a stinky pile of smelly rhino poo,
I can taste a little, tiny, delicious,
yummy bugs,
I can hear giraffes
and I can hear a lion's roar,
I can feel the wavy grass that is hot.

Casey Lennon (7)
Oak Tree Primary Academy, Mansfield

The Crocodile Of Darkness

The crocodile sees the dead body of a lion,
He smells the poo of a hyena
And sees their blood,
He tastes the flesh of a lion,
And hears the legs of a giraffe
Treading water nearby to take home.

Charlie-Lucas Koperski-Stewart (7)
Oak Tree Primary Academy, Mansfield

The Giraffe

G etting the leaves off the trees
I t is eating food
R un, giraffe!
A nd the giraffe went to sleep
F ur is yellow
F ur is brown
E ating leaves.

Katie-Leigh Hardy (6)
Oak Tree Primary Academy, Mansfield

The Giraffe

G igantic giraffe
I n Africa
R oaming around
A frican sun is hot
F inds shade to keep cool and play with
F riends
E ating the yummy leaves.

Georgia Ingram (6)
Oak Tree Primary Academy, Mansfield

The Leopard

A leopard is in the jungle
She is patterned on her body
She is fierce and furry,
She is beautiful
When she sees her food,
She creeps and gets ready
To pounce on a giraffe.

Amelia Hassan (7)
Oak Tree Primary Academy, Mansfield

Dangerous Snake

S lithering in the jungle, long grass
N asty bite, razor-sharp teeth
A iming for a
K ing cobra
E ven dangerous snakes can kill other snakes.

Jensen Charlton (7)
Oak Tree Primary Academy, Mansfield

The Monkeys

I see little monkeys in the trees.
I hear them say, "Oo oo, aa aa."
They smell like bananas and
They love the taste of bananas!
Monkeys feel so furry to touch.

Lilith Smith
Oak Tree Primary Academy, Mansfield

The Rattling Snake

A snake
I can see dark colours,
I can hear *hiss, hiss, hiss!*
I feel smooth skin,
I smell disgusting poo
And I can taste
Another squishy snake nearby.

Jessica Parker (6)
Oak Tree Primary Academy, Mansfield

The Crocodile

Crocodiles are snappy,
They can snap at any other animals
Crocodiles are green and have long tails
A loud splash wets everything nearby,
As his tail whacks the water.

Caleb Thompson (7)
Oak Tree Primary Academy, Mansfield

What Am I?

I have black and white stripes,
I have a black mane,
I have black feet,
I look like a horse,
I have four feet and four legs
I am fluffy.
What am I?

Ivy May Simpson (5)
Oak Tree Primary Academy, Mansfield

The Hyena

H yenas are spotty
Y ou can hear them
E at an elephant in the jungle
N icely hunt
A nd you might get plump, juicy food.

Keogh Turner (7)
Oak Tree Primary Academy, Mansfield

What Am I?

I have a long neck,
I have a long tail,
I have sharp teeth,
I have hooves,
I have spots,
I have long legs.
What am I?

Aiko Hallam (6)
Oak Tree Primary Academy, Mansfield

The Panda

P laying around
A nd eating lots of bamboo
N ice panda hugs
D ark paws
A nd they climb trees.

Phoebe Marie Barnett (6)
Oak Tree Primary Academy, Mansfield

What Am I?

I have black and white stripes,
I am pretty and lovely,
I look like a horse.
What am I?

Answer: A zebra. (upside down)

Jaycee-Mae Vaughan (6)
Oak Tree Primary Academy, Mansfield

What Am I?

I have black stripes,
I look like a horse,
I have a black mane.
What am I?

Answer: A zebra.

Alfie Rowley (5)
Oak Tree Primary Academy, Mansfield

What Am I?

I have black and white stripes,
I have fur,
I have hooves.
What am I?

Answer: A zebra.

Henri-Lee O'Neill (6)
Oak Tree Primary Academy, Mansfield

The Lion

L ong, sharp claws
I ncredible runner
O range mane
N oisy roar. Pounce!

Reece Simpson (6)
Oak Tree Primary Academy, Mansfield

What Am I?

I have a long tail,
I have a long neck,
I can run fast,
I have four legs
What am I?

Kaiden Radford (6)
Oak Tree Primary Academy, Mansfield

The Lion

L ong teeth
I ncredible mane
O range mane
N o baby lions.

April Marshall (6)
Oak Tree Primary Academy, Mansfield

What Am I?

I have a tail,
I have sharp teeth,
I can run fast,
I eat meat.
What am I?

Ethan O'Shea (5)
Oak Tree Primary Academy, Mansfield

What Am I?

I have black and white fur,
I have stripes,
I have a black mane.
What am I?

Liara Townsend (5)
Oak Tree Primary Academy, Mansfield

What Am I?

I have fur,
I have four legs,
I have a tail.
What am I?

Adam Hassan (6)
Oak Tree Primary Academy, Mansfield

Wintertime!

Winter looks frosty, cold and slippery,
Winter sounds like Santa's bells ringing gracefully on a cold, icy night,
Winter tastes like Christmas turkey, mince pies and Christmas pudding,
Winter smells like cold winter air and snowflakes slowly falling down,
Winter feels fluffy, soft and wet.

Sam Knifton (7)
Portway Infant School, Allestree

Superhero

A superhero is strong and cool,
A superhero is nice and fast,
A superhero is hot and magic,
A superhero is funny and smart,
A superhero is handsome and super,
A superhero is awesome and brilliant,
A superhero is invisible and caring,
A superhero is beautiful and freezes.

Caitlin Louise O'Reilly (6)
Portway Infant School, Allestree

Wintertime!

Winter looks fun but cold
Winter feels cold and frosty
but I think it's too cold,
Winter sounds like Santa's sleigh bells
dangling in the moonlight,
Winter tastes like turkey
roasting on the cooker,
Winter smells like a mince pie.

Henry Greenhalgh (7)
Portway Infant School, Allestree

Superhero

A superhero is strong and furry,
A superhero is cool and hot,
A superhero is fast and smart,
A superhero is stretchy and scary,
A superhero is nice and invisible,
A superhero is amazing and magic.

Christos Serghi (6)
Portway Infant School, Allestree

Wintertime

Winter looks frosty and icy,
Winter smells like a cold and snowy breeze blowing into my bedroom,
Winter sounds like Father Christmas passing by,
Winter tastes like Christmas pudding and turkey.

Elizabeth Ellen Hancox (7)
Portway Infant School, Allestree

Riddle

I have red, sun-bright boots,
I wear a midnight blue skirt with stars,
I am extremely powerful,
I can fly in the air.
Who am I?

Answer: Wonder Woman.

Lily White (6)
Portway Infant School, Allestree

Riddle

I have powerful lasers,
I wear red and yellow, metal armour,
I am extremely powerful,
I have glowing eyes.
Who am I?

Answer: Iron Man.

Leo Spencer (6)
Portway Infant School, Allestree

Riddle

I have green skin,
I wear purple shorts,
I am extremely strong,
I can smash buildings.
Who am I?

Answer: Hulk. (upside down)

Jack Thomas Flint (6)
Portway Infant School, Allestree

Superhero

A superhero has a mask and fire,
A superhero can flip and fly,
A superhero is cool and fast.

Oliver Curr (6)
Portway Infant School, Allestree

Giraffes
A diamante poem

Giraffes
Spotty, soft
Eyelashes, nose, neck
Munching, swinging, bending, stretching
Hooves, legs, tail
Silky, elegant
Giraffes.

Ribljot Kaur (6)
St Edward's Catholic Academy, Swadlincote

Penguin
A diamante poem

Penguin
Shiny, white
Flippers, beak, tummy
Waddling, sliding, slipping, munching
Eyes, claws, feathers
Yellow, orange
Penguin.

Amelie Struggles (6)
St Edward's Catholic Academy, Swadlincote

Octopus
A diamante poem

Octopus
Purple, clever
Tentacles, legs, gills
Swimming, curling, wiggling, gliding
Body, eyes, mouth
Slimy, wiggly
Octopus.

Charlie Gardner (5)
St Edward's Catholic Academy, Swadlincote

Octopus
A diamante poem

Octopus
Clever, slimy
Tentacles, gills, head
Swimming, eating, wiggling, twirling
Suckers, eyes, mouth
Brown, pink
Octopus.

Charlie Mole (6)
St Edward's Catholic Academy, Swadlincote

Giraffes

A diamante poem

Giraffes
Silky, beautiful
Neck, legs, tail
Swinging, bending, munching, reaching
Nose, tongue, eyes
Elegant, tail
Giraffes.

Lydia Cox (6)
St Edward's Catholic Academy, Swadlincote

Unicorns
A diamante poem

Unicorns
Fluffy, sparkly
Mane, hooves, horn
Flying, hunting, running, galloping
Tail, eyes, mouth
Rainbow, golden
Unicorns.

Bella Saddington (6)
St Edward's Catholic Academy, Swadlincote

Unicorns
A diamante poem

Unicorns
Sparkly, fluffy
Mane, horn, tail
Flying, twirling, smiling, galloping
Eyes, hooves, magic
Rainbow, cute
Unicorns.

Annemarie O'Brien (5)
St Edward's Catholic Academy, Swadlincote

Unicorns

A diamante poem

Unicorns
Rainbow, fluffy
Mane, horn, hair
Flying, dreaming, playing, hunting
Tail, smile, hooves
Magical, pretty
Unicorns.

Dollie Hutton (6)
St Edward's Catholic Academy, Swadlincote

Unicorns
A diamante poem

Unicorns
Cute, sparkly
Hooves, tail, horn
Galloping, flying, nibbling, munching
Mane, hair, smile
Golden, fluffy
Unicorn.

Layla Hallam (6)
St Edward's Catholic Academy, Swadlincote

Polar Bear
A diamante poem

Polar bear,
Big, furry
Ears, claws, teeth
Jumping, swimming, walking, diving
Tummy, fur, paws
White, sharp
Polar bear.

Jason Alexander Ogunlana (5)
St Edward's Catholic Academy, Swadlincote

Unicorns
A diamante poem

Unicorns
Gold, rainbow
Horn, tail, hooves
Dancing, running, jumping, flying
Legs, eyes, mane
Magic, fluffy,
Unicorns.

Evie-Rose Morgan (5)
St Edward's Catholic Academy, Swadlincote

Unicorns
A diamante poem

Unicorns
Pink, amazing
Hair, mane, neck
Flying, dreaming, running, nibbling
Hooves, tail, eyes
Fluffy, cute
Unicorns.

Oliver Czarkowski (6)
St Edward's Catholic Academy, Swadlincote

Unicorns
A diamante poem

Unicorns
Rainbow, fluffy
Horn, hair, mane
Jumping, dancing, running, flying
Hooves, belly, ears
Gold, cute
Unicorns.

Pixie Eyre (6)
St Edward's Catholic Academy, Swadlincote

Unicorns
A diamante poem

Fluffy, cute
Eyes, tail, horns
Eating, jogging, running, galloping
Horse, legs, horn
Cuddly, majestic
Unicorns.

Aaron Cox (5)
St Edward's Catholic Academy, Swadlincote

Summer

Summer feels like the warm, hot glimmering
sun shining and freezing cold ice cubes
Summer smells like barbecues burning
and sausages sizzling
Summer looks like children playing joyfully
and rainbows shining on them
Summer tastes like Oreo ice cream
and rainbow ice lollies
Summer sounds like people
splashing in the pool happily
And going on the galaxy water slide
And people having a water balloon fight.

Olivia Chacko (6)
St Thomas More Catholic Primary School, Kettering

Winter

Winter looks like children having snowball
fights outside in the garden with snow
Winter smells like gingerbread baking in the
hot, boiling oven
Winter tastes like roast dinner in the oven
cooking and children are waiting
Winter feels like cold air coming down on
the cold, frosty, freezing grass and trees
Winter sounds like people munching on
some warm biscuits
And crunching on some hot dinner
with hot chocolate.

Jessica Joseph (6)
St Thomas More Catholic Primary School, Kettering

Summer

Summer smells like swimming pools
splashing on the legs
in the gloomy sunshine
Summer looks like a rainbow
flying across the sky
Summer tastes like a pizza
burning in a burner
Summer feels like air
wafting across the face of you
Summer sounds like angels coming down
and waving in the bright blue,
glistening sky.

Maizie Ielapi (7)
St Thomas More Catholic Primary School, Kettering

Winter

Winter feels like cold and icy places
Winter looks like Santa
coming out of the chimney
Winter feels like Santa bringing presents
Winter smells like hot gingerbread baking
Winter smells like yummy biscuits
Winter sounds like people
playing in the park
Winter looks like my friends coming outside
to my house to play with me.

Christa Bijumon (6)
St Thomas More Catholic Primary School, Kettering

Summer

Summer looks like ladies dancing
on the smooth sand
Summer smells like lovely hot dogs
and scrumptious burgers
leaving delicious crumbs
Summer tastes like delicious burgers
steaming on the hot barbecue
Summer feels like the refreshing, cool sea
Summer sounds like happy children
playing under the bright, hot sun.

Sienna Palmiero (6)
St Thomas More Catholic Primary School, Kettering

Summer

Summer looks like doing sprinklers
Summer smells like sausages
Summer tastes like ice lollies
Summer feels like people
Playing in the swimming pool
Summer sounds like people singing happily
Summer sounds like people dancing happily
Summer feels like people lying down
Summer looks like people dancing well.

Rosemaria Jiju (6)
St Thomas More Catholic Primary School, Kettering

Winter

Winter tastes like lovely, fresh tasty
Christmas dinner
Winter sounds like children laughing in joy
Winter feels like special snow
that melts on you like magic
Winter looks like shiny snow
falling down like birds
Winter smells like Christmas dinner
and Christmas pudding,
like a combination for love.

Gerard Rony (7)
St Thomas More Catholic Primary School, Kettering

Autumn

Autumn looks like people eating popcorn in
the cold, dark and spooky night
Autumn smells like popping candy
and burgers
Autumn tastes like children eating
toffee apples and doughnuts
Autumn feels like hot dogs
sizzling in my mouth
Autumn sounds like children
giggling in the frosty air.

Grace Claypole (7)
St Thomas More Catholic Primary School, Kettering

Summer

Summer looks like people
splashing in the sea with joy
Summer smells like big, hot burgers
on the barbecue
Summer tastes like yummy hot dogs
with ketchup and mayonnaise
Summer feels like the cool pool
with lots of people in it
Summer sounds like kids
swimming happily in the pool.

Camron Gerard Mills (7)
St Thomas More Catholic Primary School, Kettering

Awesome Autumn

Autumn looks like curly Catherine wheels
and fluffy candyfloss
Autumn smells like an appetising hot
chocolate and tossing leaves
Autumn tastes like mouthwatering hot dogs
with a yummy ketchup dip
Autumn feels like warm, cosy
and fluffy ear muffs
Autumn sounds like crackling,
fizzling fireworks.

Betsy Flannigan (7)
St Thomas More Catholic Primary School, Kettering

Summer

Summer looks like people
having water balloon fights
Summer smells like people cooking burgers
Summer sounds like people
splashing in the pool loudly
Summer tastes like delicious,
appetising ice cream
And tasty lollies
Summer sounds like people
splashing in the pool.

Luke Rahman (7)
St Thomas More Catholic Primary School, Kettering

Summer

Summer tastes like people eating
strawberry ice cream and chocolate
Summer sounds like people
splashing in the pool
Summer feels like a nice, warm, fun time
Summer smells like nice
cut grass and flowers
Summer looks like people having water
balloon fights in shorts and laughing.

Oliver Kopaniecki (6)
St Thomas More Catholic Primary School, Kettering

Summer

Summer tastes like delicious ice cream with sprinkles and rainbow slushies
Summer smells like freshly cut grass and barbecues
Summer looks like children swimming and diving
Summer feels hot and sunny
Summer sounds like children splashing in the sparkly water.

Amelia Jino (7)
St Thomas More Catholic Primary School, Kettering

Summer

Summer looks like people in hot tubs
and in swimsuits and a disco
Summer smells like barbecue smoke
Summer tastes like burgers
and sausages burning
Summer feels like fun waterslides
and waterparks
Summer sounds like children
laughing happily.

Aurelia Curtis (6)
St Thomas More Catholic Primary School, Kettering

Spring

Spring looks like beautiful blossoms
growing on the trees
Spring smells like fresh air in your face
Spring tastes like yummy hotdogs
on the barbecue
Spring feels like smooth birch on the trees
Spring sounds like children
giggling with happiness.

Sean Prendergast (7)
St Thomas More Catholic Primary School, Kettering

Winter

Winter sounds like laughing
in the glittery snow falling down
Winter feels like the crunch of leaves
Winter tastes like the hot chocolate
burning in your mouth
Winter smells like nature everywhere!
Winter looks like children
playing in the snow.

Amelia Alexander (7)
St Thomas More Catholic Primary School, Kettering

Winter

Winter looks like shiny frost shimmering
and fluffy snow
Winter smells like ice cubes and lemonade
Winter tastes like warm roast dinner
and yummy chocolate putting
Winter feels like freezing toes frozen
Winter sounds like winds blowing coldly.

Esha Rijo Joseph (6)
St Thomas More Catholic Primary School, Kettering

Autumn

Autumn looks like brown and yellow leaves
Autumn tastes like yummy popcorn
and toffee apples
Autumn feels like crunchy brown leaves
Autumn smells like fresh pink
and purple doughnuts
Autumn sounds like fizzing
and popping barbecues.

Matilda Vincitore-Jackson (6)
St Thomas More Catholic Primary School, Kettering

Summer

Summer looks like the sun gleaming warm
Summer smells like people
cooking sausages outside
Summer tastes like cookies for pudding
Summer feels like paddling pools
in the warm sun
Summer sounds like children
giggling at the movies.

Oscar Arden-Taylor (7)
St Thomas More Catholic Primary School, Kettering

Winter

Winter looks like children
having fun in the snow
Winter smells like chicken cooking
Winter tastes like coldness
flying all around us
Winter feels like us making snow angels
Winter sounds like snow
falling down to the ground.

William Richardson (6)
St Thomas More Catholic Primary School, Kettering

Summer

Summer looks like people eating ice cream
And the sun shining
Summer tastes like people
eating delicious hot dogs
Summer sounds like people
laughing happily
Summer feels like hot weather
Summer smells like fresh grass.

Cyprian Leatherland (6)
St Thomas More Catholic Primary School, Kettering

Summer

Summer looks like children
playing in the waters
Summer smells like sea and sand
Summer tastes like bubblegum ice cream
Summer feels like a very hot day
Summer sounds like children
splashing in the swimming pool.

Seth James Stanyon (7)
St Thomas More Catholic Primary School, Kettering

Summer

Summer looks like little kids surfing
Summer smells like a barbecue
Summer tastes like a cool ice cream
Summer feels like a hot, sunny day
Summer sounds like little children
laughing and splashing in a cool pool.

Lily Driscoll (6)
St Thomas More Catholic Primary School, Kettering

Winter

Winter looks like people getting cold
Winter looks like gingerbread baking
Winter looks like people eating
roast dinners
Winter looks like children playing
in the snow
Winter looks like it is silent.

Joel Binoy (6)
St Thomas More Catholic Primary School, Kettering

Summer

Summer looks like children having fun
Summer smells like fresh grass
Summer tastes like ice cream
Summer feels like warm weather
Summer sounds like people
Having ice in their drink.

Maria Mucaj (6)
St Thomas More Catholic Primary School, Kettering

Summer

Summer smells like yummy burgers
Summer feels like warm sun
Summer sounds like kids laughing so loud
Summer looks like kids eating ice lollies
Summer tastes like bubblegum ice cream.

Mia Drappo (7)
St Thomas More Catholic Primary School, Kettering

Summer

Summer looks like children
Spraying water guns
Summer smells like barbecues
Summer feels like sandcastles
Summer tastes like ice cream
Summer sounds like the swimming pool.

Mini Holder (6)
St Thomas More Catholic Primary School, Kettering

Winter

Winter sounds like Santa ringing the bell
Winter smells like Christmas dinners
Winter feels like freezing ice
Winter sounds like snowballs
Winter looks like snowflakes.

Oliver Wise (7)
St Thomas More Catholic Primary School, Kettering

Cheetahs

Cheetahs sound loud
Cheetahs smell like flowers
Cheetahs taste like hay
Cheetahs sound like tigers
Cheetahs feel like a rabbit
Cheetahs look strong.

Lottie Tyler (6)
Sutherland Primary Academy, Blurton

Smelly Zebras

Zebras sound like a herd of chimpanzees
Zebras taste like gammon and lamb
Zebras smell stinky and grassy
Zebras feel nice
Zebras look stripy.

Zachary S (6)
Sutherland Primary Academy, Blurton

Zebras

Zebras sound really loud
Zebras taste like Peperami
Zebras smell like grass
Zebras feel as hard as a brick
Zebras look stripy and hairy.

Ethan Morris (5)
Sutherland Primary Academy, Blurton

Tiger Poem

Tigers sound like roaring cats
Tigers taste yucky and muddy
Tigers feel soft and smooth
Tigers smell of sticky meat
Tigers look stripy.

Lacey-Mae S (5)
Sutherland Primary Academy, Blurton

Elephant Poem

Elephants sound like loud trumpets
Elephants taste like disgusting mud
Elephants smell pooey
Elephants feel rough
Elephants look giant.

Poppy C (5)
Sutherland Primary Academy, Blurton

Elephant Poem

Elephants sound like loud trumpets
Elephants taste like disgusting mud
Elephants smell pooey
Elephants feel rough
Elephants look light.

John V (6)
Sutherland Primary Academy, Blurton

Zebra

A zebra smells disgusting
A zebra feels hard
A zebra looks stripy and white
A zebra tastes like grass and yucky
A zebra sounds quiet.

Adam W (6)
Sutherland Primary Academy, Blurton

Giraffe Poem

Giraffes sound loud and squeaky
Giraffes taste yucky
Giraffes smell grassy
Giraffes feel soft and hairy
Giraffes look big and long.

Aiden B (6)
Sutherland Primary Academy, Blurton

Cheetah

Cheetahs are quiet
Cheetahs taste like mud
Cheetahs are muddy
Cheetahs smell nice
Cheetahs feel soft
Cheetahs look pillowy.

Brooke R (5)
Sutherland Primary Academy, Blurton

Cheetah Senses

Cheetahs sound like a growling cat
Cheetahs taste yucky
Cheetahs smell muddy
Cheetahs feel soft and fluffy
Cheetahs look skinny.

Emily F (5)
Sutherland Primary Academy, Blurton

Tiger Senses

Tigers sound like a growling cat
Tigers tasty like meat
Tigers smell like muddy grass
Tigers feel furry
Tigers look stripy.

Harry William Shaw (5)
Sutherland Primary Academy, Blurton

Tiger

Tigers sound as loud as a rocket
Tigers taste disgusting
Tigers smell like clean meat
Tigers feel soft
Tigers look stripy.

Oliver Lawrence (5)
Sutherland Primary Academy, Blurton

Cheetahs

Cheetahs sound like *meow!*
Cheetahs taste like mud
Cheetahs smell stinky
Cheetahs look sneaky
Cheetahs feel soft.

Lilly H R (5)
Sutherland Primary Academy, Blurton

Elephant

Elephants sound like trumpets
Elephants taste like meat
Elephants smell like grass
Elephants feel smooth
Elephants look grey.

Tala H (6)
Sutherland Primary Academy, Blurton

Cheetahs

A cheetah sounds quiet
A cheetah tastes muddy
A cheetah smells stinky
A cheetah feels cuddly
A cheetah looks like a cat.

Jaxon P (6)
Sutherland Primary Academy, Blurton

Tiger

A tiger sounds noisy
A tiger tastes furry
A tiger smells like meat
A tiger feels as soft as a bear
A tiger looks stripy.

Rory G (5)
Sutherland Primary Academy, Blurton

Giraffes

Giraffes sound loud
Giraffes taste like chocolate
Giraffes smell disgusting
Giraffes feel smooth
Giraffes look big.

Jayden Derek Bennett (5)
Sutherland Primary Academy, Blurton

Giraffes' Five Senses

Giraffes sound loud
Giraffes taste yucky
Giraffes smell grassy
Giraffes feel hairy
Giraffes look long and big.

Charlie W (6)
Sutherland Primary Academy, Blurton

Giraffe Poem

Giraffes look long and big
Giraffes feel soft
Giraffes tasty yucky
Giraffes sound loud
Giraffes smell grassy.

Riley O'Connell (6)
Sutherland Primary Academy, Blurton

Cheetahs

Cheetahs sound really noisy
Cheetahs taste mud
Cheetahs smell yucky
Cheetahs feel soft
Cheetahs look chunky.

Ruby (5)
Sutherland Primary Academy, Blurton

Zebra Senses

Zebras sound like horses
Zebras taste like meat
Zebras smell muddy
Zebras feel soft
Zebras look stripy.

Amelia E (6)
Sutherland Primary Academy, Blurton

Giraffe

Giraffes sound loud
Giraffes taste sweet
Giraffes smell dirty
Giraffes feel hard
Giraffes look yellow.

Emmanuel Chiagozelam U (6)
Sutherland Primary Academy, Blurton

Tigers Sound Like

Tigers taste hairy
Tigers smell furry
Tigers feel soft
Tigers look stripy
Tigers sound like a big cat.

Lilly Iris Bowman (6)
Sutherland Primary Academy, Blurton

Tigers Sound Like

Tigers sound like loud cats
Tigers taste hairy
Tigers smell muddy
Tigers feel soft
Tigers look scary!

Leo G (5)
Sutherland Primary Academy, Blurton

Zebra

Zebras sound loud
Zebras taste hard
Zebras feel cold
Zebras look big
Zebras smell like grass.

Jenson-Edward L (6)
Sutherland Primary Academy, Blurton

Tigers

Tigers sound loud
Tigers taste hairy
Tigers smell furry
Tigers feel soft
Tigers look stripy.

Trystan A (6)
Sutherland Primary Academy, Blurton

Giraffe

Giraffes sound loud
Giraffes smell like chocolate cake
Giraffes feel smooth
Giraffes look yellow.

Karolina Kovacovska (6)
Sutherland Primary Academy, Blurton

Zebra

A zebra sounds loud
A zebra smells smelly
A zebra feels cold and warm
A zebra looks big.

Jacob Heath-Willis (5)
Sutherland Primary Academy, Blurton

Giraffe

Giraffes sound loud
Giraffes taste yucky
Giraffes smell like trees
Giraffes feel smooth.

Harrison G (5)
Sutherland Primary Academy, Blurton

Elephant Poem

Elephants sound noisy
Elephants smell stinky
Elephants feel rough
Elephants look huge.

Zakariya H (5)
Sutherland Primary Academy, Blurton

Giraffes

Giraffes taste yummy
Giraffes smell dirty
Giraffes feel nice
Giraffes look big.

Stanley William-Booth Cook (6)
Sutherland Primary Academy, Blurton

Princess Dreams

P retty in pink and purple, playing in the palace
R iding a rainbow unicorn around the royal rose bushes
I mportant things to do indoors, imagining I'm invisible and having ice cream
N ice new necklaces and never being naughty
C ounting chocolate coins, cuddling cute cats and cleaning my crown
E ating eggs for breakfast and enjoying exciting events
S inging sweet songs, wearing sparkly shoes
S leeping under the stars, keeping special secrets.

Sophie Stamp-Broadway (6)
West Heath Primary School, West Heath

The Beach

The beach is my favourite place to go,
I always pack a beachball to throw
I enjoy swimming in the sea,
I go so deep, you can hardly see me
I always take a bucket and spade
And show everyone the castles I've made
I have ice cream to cool me down,
If I don't like the flavour, I will frown
It's sad when I have to go home,
I wish I could stay here on my own
Why do I have to pack away?
There is so much more I want to play!

Lily Grace Fay (6)
West Heath Primary School, West Heath

Wonderful Winter

Winter looks like sparkling ice
shining on the floor
Winter sounds like a wolf howling
as the wind blows on your face
Winter smells like yummy cookies
baking in the oven
Winter feels icy cold
as it pinches your fingers and toes
Winter tastes like warm hot chocolate
making you feel happy
Winter is my favourite time of the year.

Mollie Johnson (6)
West Heath Primary School, West Heath

My Pug Dog Teddy

I have a puppy
He used to be jumpy
But now he is grumpy
When I get home from school,
He thinks it's cool
We can't wait to go on walks
And eat our food with knives and forks
When me and my puppy go on walks,
I wish he could talk
I wonder what he would say
If he is like me,
He would talk all day!

Katie Irene Tonks (7)
West Heath Primary School, West Heath

I Love Football

F ield ready, football on the spot
O ff we go
O ver the bar, how did I miss?
T ime to try again
B lock and tackle, to keep the ball
A wesome teamwork
L eap and header into the goal
L ove football, it's so much fun!

Kyle Smith (6)
West Heath Primary School, West Heath

What Animal Am I Guessing?

I am long and scaly,
I have a long, red tongue
I eat bugs and I am green
I am also quite wide
I live in a pond and on a lily pad
I am almost as sneaky as a snake
Catching my prey
Can you guess what I am?

Lexi Painter (7)
West Heath Primary School, West Heath

The Wrestler Roman Reigns

Roman Reigns looks like a beast
Roman Reigns sounds like Hulk,
Roman Reigns smells like sweat,
Roman Reigns feels like a muscle man,
Roman Reigns tastes like meat,
Roman Reigns is always on his feet.

Rehan Ahmed (7)
West Heath Primary School, West Heath

The Seasons

Hats, scarves and gloves
In winter, we make snow angels
Blossom, butterflies and lambs
In spring, we go to the farm
Sandcastles, sunglasses and ice cream
In summer, we build sandcastles
In summer, we go to the beach
Acorns, leaves and brown
In autumn, we jump in the crunchy leaves.

Sophie Mafuamba (5)
Yardley Wood Community Primary School, Yardley Wood

The Seasons

Sprouts, turkey and Christmas
In winter, we have a snowball fight
Blossom, frog spawn and flowers
In spring, we have an Easter hunt in gardens
Sandcastles and swimming
In summer, we go swimming
Pumpkins, leaves and harvest
In autumn, we listen to the fireworks.

Kenzie Taylor (6)
Yardley Wood Community Primary School, Yardley Wood

Seasons

Snowball fight, Christmas and snowmen
In winter, we drink hot chocolate
Flowers, blossom and ducklings
In spring, we see things grow
Holidays, ice cream and hot
In summer, we go to the seaside
Squirrels, conkers and pumpkins
In autumn, we kick the leaves about.

Lillie Evans (6)
Yardley Wood Community Primary School, Yardley Wood

Seasons

Coats, ice and freezing
In winter, we can have a snowball fight
Chicks, flowers and lambs
In spring, we can see things grow
Sun, beach and hats
In summer, we can go to the beach
Acorns, pumpkins and leaves
In autumn, we can kick the leaves.

Hunaida Suwan (6)
Yardley Wood Community Primary School, Yardley Wood

The Seasons

Sprouts, crackers and snowballs
In winter, we can build a snowman
Flowers, chicks and buds
In spring, we catch butterflies
Ice cream, sun and suncream
In summer, we eat ice cream
Oak, Halloween and pumpkins
In autumn, we watch fireworks.

Mohammed Hussnain (6)
Yardley Wood Community Primary School, Yardley Wood

The Seasons

Hot chocolate, snowmen and snowflakes
In winter, we make snow angels
Chicks, lambs and blossom
In spring, we can go to the farm
Sun, sun hat and beach
In summer, we eat ice cream
Pumpkin, scarecrows and rakes
In autumn, we see squirrels.

Dexter Hollingsworth (6)
Yardley Wood Community Primary School, Yardley Wood

The Seasons

Scarf, hat and Santa
In winter, we build a snowman
Easter eggs, rain and blossom
In spring, we play with butterflies
Sun, ice cream and aeroplanes
In summer, we go to the beach
Beech, oak and sycamore
In autumn, we look at the trees.

Isla Burton (5)
Yardley Wood Community Primary School, Yardley Wood

The Seasons

Scarves, hats and gloves
In the winter, we play in the snow
Farm, lamb and blossom
In spring, we can go to the farm
Hot, ice cream and plane
In summer, we can play on the beach
Oak, leaves and harvest
In autumn, we jump in leaves.

Ibraheem Farrell (5)
Yardley Wood Community Primary School, Yardley Wood

Seasons

Scarves, gloves and hats
In winter, we go ice skating
Chicks, lambs and flowers
In spring, we see tadpoles
Holidays, beach and sandcastles
In summer, we eat ice cream
Pumpkins, acorns and leaves
In autumn, we kick the leaves.

Toby Page (6)
Yardley Wood Community Primary School, Yardley Wood

The Seasons

Gloves, hat and sledging
In winter, we have snowball fights
Chicks, rain and flowers
In spring, we see tadpoles
Sun hat, sun and ice cream
In summer, we go to the beach
Rake, oak and tree
In autumn, we jump in the leaves.

Salah-Eddin Melloul (6)
Yardley Wood Community Primary School, Yardley Wood

The Seasons

Snowman, hot chocolate and hat
In winter, we build a snowman
Rain, lambs and tadpoles
In spring, we go to the farm
Sun, beach and tents
In summer, we go to the beach
Tree, oak and rake
In autumn, we play in the leaves.

Laibaah Khan (5)
Yardley Wood Community Primary School, Yardley Wood

The Seasons

Snowman, hat and hot chocolate
In winter, we play in the snow
Flowers, lambs and chicks
In spring, we feed lambs
Sunny, hats and holidays
In summer, we go on holiday
Oak, rake and tree
In autumn, we grow pumpkins.

Kaéson Gaye-Smith (6)
Yardley Wood Community Primary School, Yardley Wood

The Seasons

Squirrels, leaves and trees
In autumn, we can lie in the leaves
Hat, scarf and gloves
In winter, we can build a snowman
Lambs, butterflies and blossom
In spring, we can go to the farm.

Paige Lake (6)
Yardley Wood Community Primary School, Yardley Wood

The Seasons

In winter, we can have a snowball fight
In spring, we can feed the lambs
In summer, we can eat ice cream
In autumn, we kick the leaves.

Ethan Hourihan (5)
Yardley Wood Community Primary School, Yardley Wood

Seasons

In winter, we can build snowmen
In spring, we can feed the ducks
In autumn, we can trick or treat.

Rylee Mottram (5)
Yardley Wood Community Primary School, Yardley Wood

Summer

Summer is here
Summer is gone
Summer is hot
Summer has arrived
Summer is beautiful
Summer is the best season of the year
Summer is always shiny
Summer is never raining
Summer is the best season
Summer is fun
Summer is coming to down.

Saaliha Mahmood (6)
Yorkmead School, Hall Green

Who Am I?

I like to wear a big, red coat,
I have an important job to do on an eve,
I can live in a frost place,
I can fly in the sky,
I have eight magnificent reindeer
And a beard as white as snow
Who am I?

Answer: Santa Claus.

Haseeb Abdul (7)
Yorkmead School, Hall Green

Young Writers Information

We hope you have enjoyed reading this book – and that you will continue to in the coming years.

If you're a young writer who enjoys reading and creative writing, or the parent of an enthusiastic poet or story writer, do visit our website **www.youngwriters.co.uk**. Here you will find free competitions, workshops and games, as well as recommended reads, a poetry glossary and our blog.

If you would like to order further copies of this book, or any of our other titles, then please give us a call or visit **www.youngwriters.co.uk**.

Young Writers
Remus House
Coltsfoot Drive
Peterborough
PE2 9BF
(01733) 890066
info@youngwriters.co.uk

@YoungWritersUK @YoungWritersCW